AIRMAIL

A STORY OF WAR IN POEMS

KATHLEEN PATRICK

Copyright 2022 by Kathleen Patrick Terhaar

CONTENTS

Note from the Author	v
Letter to Seven Uncles	1
I. LEAVING	3
Photo Interpreter	4
Chain Link	7
Bad Time	10
Letter from Ed	14
Kent State or Whose Poem is this Anyway?	15
When the Wind's from the North	17
Heavy Load	20
Judy	22
Mother Wept	24
Little Sis	26
Aftermath	28
Telegram	32
Uncle Eddie Builds a House	33
Robert M. in the Doorway	36
II. AIRMAIL	39
Voices, A Collage	40
III. SURVIVING	71
First Born	72
Brother on Leave	74
Love, Colleen	76
Picking Rock	78
Smoke on the Water	80
I'm Taller, Tim	82
Christmas Leave	84
Write Soon	86
Funny Money	88
Decisions	90
Survivor	92
Interview with Dee	94
Silk Dragons	97
Clem	99

Don't Forget the Women	101
The Youngest One	103
Lost Records	105
BB Guns	108
Brothers in Arms at Quang Tri	112
Mississippi Morning	115
Cowboy in Alaska	118
Talking to Angels	120
Sharp Shooter	122
Follow Up	124
Acknowledgments	127
About the Author	129
Thank You	131
Please Review This Book!	133

NOTE FROM THE AUTHOR

When I was in the fourth grade, we had a map of Vietnam on our kitchen wall. When my mother received an airmail letter, she would walk to the map and move one of the stickpins to a new location to see if one of her brothers was in harm's way in some new hot spot or battle. I spent a lot of time worrying about that map. I had five uncles in Southeast Asia during the Vietnam War. Looking back, I guess it is a bit unusual for a girl of nine or ten to write letters to her uncles in Vietnam, in Thailand, in Cambodia. Even then, I knew that words could make one feel better. I wrote about ice-skating at the park on a cold Iowa Saturday. I wrote about school, basketball games, and the books I was reading. My letters were written in wide, awkward printing on little girl stationary. My uncles wrote back and thanked me for writing.

Several years ago, one of those uncles wrote a line at the bottom of his Christmas card. It said, "Someday I want to sit down and tell you what it was like to be a young man going off to war." I taped that card over my desk and began to imagine their voices. Over the next years, I read hundreds of letters that my mother and my grandfather had saved from the boys, spanning many years. With the help of a Jerome Foundation Grant and a Loft McKnight grant, I visited several of the men in Mississippi, Alaska, and South Dakota and interviewed them about their experiences. I recalled stories from my childhood. They filled in the details. Some preferred not to talk about it; others felt like it had released a great burden.

This manuscript is the result of those letters and those stories. It is a book about going off to war, a book about coming back home, and a book about those who are left behind. I took a few liberties with the facts simply because I do not know all there is to know, but I tried to retain the voices I have heard my whole life, the voices that ring true on parchment paper sent in airmail letters from all over the world.

I dedicate this book to those voices, to my family, and every voice calling out at times of war: "I miss you. I love you. I wish I was home."

DEDICATION

*This book is dedicated to
Erma Young Smith, Joseph Edward Smith,
and their children.*

Colleen Mae Smith Patrick. b. September 20, 1936

*William Henry Smith b. October 12, 1937
United States Navy
United States Air Force*

*Charles Leroy Smith. b. January 21, 1939 d. August 22, 1992
United States Marines
United States Army*

*Clement James Smith b. June 15, 1942. d. May 15, 2021
United States Navy*

*Robert Michael Smith b. January 27, 1944
United States Navy*

Edward Joseph Smith b. July 17, 1945 d. March 5, 2014
United States Army

Judith Faye Smith. b. November 30, 1946

Terrance David Smith b. September 22, 1951
United States Air Force

Delores Rae Smith Anderson b. November 29, 1953

Timothy Allen Smith b. March 21, 1956
United States Army

LETTER TO SEVEN UNCLES

Do you remember the smell of Lava soap

in the front porch when Dee and I sang "The Cruel War"?

Eddie's stern face in the mirror

when we sang his name instead of Johnny,

sang for your tears and the ceremony of good-bye?

Do you remember the coffee cans full of candy bars,

cookies and Dentine gum? Those CARE packages

from your mother's yellow kitchen

in the quiet days before the harvest?

I REMEMBER the map of Vietnam

on our kitchen wall in Iowa.

Each morning Mom listened to the news,

read blue airmail letters,

and moved stick pins from one place

to another. I was nine and wanted

to stop that color-by-number war.

GRANDMA WROTE to each of you every week.
She stood outside on the steps
when you came home on leave. Every time
you drove into that yard.
Always outside waiting.
There is no one at the door now,
no one standing on the stoop
when the cars drive in or out.
And what of that?
What of the long nights
when you tried to make sense
of a blank sheet of paper? Tried to think
of something safe to say?
Maybe I am standing at the door now.
I don't know what to say, but
I think it is important to write it down.
What do you remember?
What are you willing to tell?

I. LEAVING

PHOTO INTERPRETER

I made sense of it
from the skies of Vietnam, looking down.

Above the menacing canopy

there was still all that sky

and God seemed, I don't know, closer.

It was my job to ferret out

the next disaster before it blew.

Photo mapping, target analysis,

bomb damage assessment.

I reported to Westmoreland each morning,

read those photographs, hell,

like a Gypsy reads an old man's palm.

                                . . .

Guess I was an expert at reading war from the sky.

But I tell you, I remember this one B-52 strike.

I was doing BDA, working my way through a bomb train;

I could see people standing around a crater,

could see the pattern of a building -- the bomb

made a direct hit on a house. I saw

villagers standing around this gaping hole--

little kids stood next to parents

and hugged their unsteady legs.

I mean those kids looked like photos in my wallet.

That night, black and white glossies

floated over my bed,

ghosts that wouldn't go away.

I saw the high school newspaper,

the square Brownie camera that Sis used

to shoot the basketball team.

"We're weak at the corner of the court,"

I told her over breakfast eggs

and homemade bread.

"I see a truck park half-a-mile from the border

but can't make out the intruding machinery."

"Follow the river," Sis said

with the gauzy voice of a dream.

"Let the shadows enhance the image."

CHAIN LINK

Brother Bill was getting off a plane--
just in from Nam and I was going out.
Kadena Air Force Base. Okinawa.
Kind of strange that we met there like that
on the tarmac, he in the Air Force and me the Navy--
two brothers in with hundreds, hell thousands,
of soldiers coming and going.
I was looking around, waiting in line,
you do that a lot in the service,
watching them unload aluminum coffins
off this big C141 cargo plane
and then I saw Bill.
I wasn't that worried about being shipped out.

I'd been in a long time already;

I thought I was invincible -- you know?

But, then I saw Bill and I knew for the first time,

just one look at his face -- what I was in for

over there. They kept pulling those coffins

off the plane on pallets stacked five high.

I mean there's a hundred dead kids --

right there in one neat little pile;

they just shoved them out the back of that plane.

Two minutes, a hundred more and bam!

the plane's empty and taxis away in a hurry.

Bill runs over to me,

sticks his fingers through the chain link,

his line of men going one way

and mine going the other.

"Jesus Christ Bobby, it's good to see you."

And then there's this long pause and his eyes

go right through me.

"Just keep your head down little brother

and you'll be all right, you hear me?

Keep your head god damn on the ground."

Kind of funny, when you think about it.

Two farm boys a long way from home

standing at what could be the gates of hell--

touching each other's fingers

to be sure we're both alive.

BAD TIME

Trapped in the distance between a photograph
and the truth, we sit at his retired table,
look over Vietnam, spread before us in living color.
Look at three friends standing by a duck boat in Iran,
a blonde woman he almost loved in Helsinki.
His first crew in Moscow.

> *The service was*
> *my mistress.*
> *I loved her. It was*
> *a good life. But Vietnam? . . .*
> *Vietnam was . . .*

He looks at the tape recorder, looks
at me looking at him. Goes to the fridge
for more ice for his Coke.

I see the snapshot of the tiger,

strung up, stretching thirteen feet,

blood dripping onto the Vietnamese sand.

Bob stands next to it, at ease with his rifle.

I remember this picture, go back

to the kitchen in South Dakota,

everyone around the table listening to his letter.

> *The tiger leapt from the woods*
> *and grabbed a Marine*
> *walking boarder patrol, grabbed him*
> *by the neck*
> *like a cat with a mouse.*
> *I mean there were twenty soldiers*
> *walking in line on that patrol*
> *and two seconds and it was over.*
> *Can you imagine?*
> *Since the perimeter was secure,*
> *we formed a search party there,*
> *and closed in the circle, trapping it.*

I hold the image and ask another question.

Weren't you afraid to walk through the jungle?

> *What do you mean?*

Didn't you feel vulnerable to the Viet Cong?

He smiles, takes a drink and leans back in his chair.

> *I didn't think about Charlie once.*

> *We were almost happy.*
> *This was hunting; this was an escape.*
> *We knew who we were after. We knew*
> *how to win this one.*

They found and killed the tiger.

Found the bones

of fourteen others, bones in a cave

where the tiger fed.

> *It was their territory. The whole area*
> *a game refuge before the war.*
> *Now they were being napalmed*
> *and driven into madness.*

I remember hearing that letter,

feeling for the first time

how far away Vietnam was:

there were tigers in the jungle. I felt

a dense humidity

trapped near my skin. A danger more real

than NBC's correspondent war talk.

> *Of course, that news*
> *didn't go home to the boy's family;*
> *he was killed in battle*
> *defending his country, there were*
> *so many killed in tragic, senseless*
> *ways unrelated to the war.*

He tells me about the fragging of officers

by their own men:

when a grenade goes off under a sergeant's bed

because he has crossed over,

he has lost contact with reality and let fear

control his every order, his need to hide

all day in his bunker.

His fear becomes the new enemy.

His death-- a mere casualty of war.

He tells me this across twenty-five years,

finally able to speak, his voice completely controlled.

> *I want you to know*
> *I'm not telling any secrets here.*
> *Now I can read all about this stuff*
> *in Newsweek or Time.*

I remember thinking that you were the one

who shot the tiger, I say.

I told my friends

that you'd shot a tiger in Vietnam.

Were you the one who killed it?

> *No, I wasn't,*
> *but we all hunted it down,*
> *and we were all glad it was dead.*

LETTER FROM ED

My twenty years in the service? I found my beautiful wife there. Best thing that ever happened to me.

There's nothing else to tell.

KENT STATE OR WHOSE POEM IS THIS ANYWAY?

One says Kent State
should have been a national holiday

TO SHOCK me I suspect

but I know now he means it

NOT THAT WE should remember the dead

not that kind of holiday

WHEN YOUR COUNTRY calls

you answer

YOU DON'T MAKE judgments is this

a good war a just war you just go

I TRY to ignore it

some things are better left but he says

I DON'T SEE my Kent State comment

anywhere in your poems and I say

NO YOU DON'T NEVER INTENDING

for any of it to end up in a poem

WHEN THE WIND'S FROM THE NORTH

When the wind's from the East,
the fish bite least.
When the wind's from the West,
the fish bite best.
When the wind's from the South,
it blows the hook in their mouth.
-Unknown

Since you asked me, I've been gathering

those years like baiting hooks and

pulling them in one by one.

I remember uniforms. Big brothers

home on leave in dress whites

or green wool and shiny shoes. Every night

at the kitchen table they buffed those

black shoes. On Sunday,

Mom beamed as she led us all

into the pew at church.

Home from Nam. Korea. Moscow. Iran.

"Two weeks leave," she'd whisper

to the neighbor behind us "then it's over there."

Later she'd sit in her rocker and write letters

to all the other boys. Army, Navy, Marines.

Her boys. Seven of them. She wrote information

gently easing into the gap

between the continents, between

all that she knew and all that was missing.

New calves. One-and-a-quarter-inches of rain

Tuesday. Corn looks good.

AND WHEN I WAS OLDER,

how many points I'd scored against Elkton,

what our record was for the season.

The brother who was home on leave

would take us little ones to town for candy

and pop and sometimes,

I'd catch a funny look on his face,

like he had a rock in his shoe or his ears hurt,

but he'd smile and walk proud.

My older brothers were always in uniform

when they went to town.

And before they went back,

before their time was up,

Dad would take us all fishing.

Fried chicken and homemade bread.

I'd sit there, watching my big brother,

watching my line in the water,

and wonder when it

would be my turn.

Untangling fears and longing

like a cast gone bad

and snagged in a tree.

HEAVY LOAD

Sometimes you just had to laugh or you couldn't go on. Somebody would say, "Well, that dumb bastard deserved to get blown up, I mean, what was he picking

that shiny shit up off the ground for anyway?"

Like that. And sometimes the war would seem pretty damn funny.

I remember this one time we were all standing

around after some pretty devastating shit.

Standing around feeling hollow and heavy and

we see this helicopter flying over Hill 12 or 26,

or whatever, and it's got a load of two-by-four's

in its sling, and then another flies over

with another load of lumber, and then

a third bird has a jeep in its sling

and the helicopter starts looking a little

unsteady and shimmies back and forth and

all of a sudden it's really swaying and that jeep

slips out of the sling and falls.

We watch it hit the ground, all of us together,

and it hits and I swear bounces thirty feet

back up in the air and the second time

it hits we all break up laughing. Laughing

at a jeep in a fireball.

You know? Crazy shit.

But then we all take a breath,

look over our shoulders and get on with it.

JUDY

The one God blessed most of all.
The life-long child, the jigsaw puzzle
no one had figured out.
She could make breakfast
and dress herself, hang chambray shirts
on the clothesline.
She could write letters on flowered stationary
to all of her missing brothers.

> *How are you? I am fine.*
> *It is hot today.*
> *Mom take me to town. I write*
> *this letter all by myself. Write soon.*

She didn't ponder the war. Her brothers
came home and left again. She went to school

and learned her letters,

until the last day of first grade

when the teacher sent her home with a note.

> *Don't send Judy back next year.*
> *There's no more we can do for her.*

After that, she became her mother's shadow,

her helper in the kitchen,

her headache some days,

her spark when the fire was already too hot.

MOTHER WEPT

Mother wept when Kennedy died.
Sat down in her rocker in the living room
with pen and paper and addressed an envelope
to a son in Vietnam.
Said son,
I've lost someone I love.
I dreamed last night that it was spring,
that you were still a baby
and I rocked and rocked you
in the midnight quiet.
The smell of apple blossoms
came in through the screens.
It was so real that when I woke up
I listened for your cry.

Are you all right?

I . . . we all miss you.

Stay safe and pray

for the recovery of a country

as I pray each night for you.

LITTLE SIS

Oh, I remember being afraid of them,
strangers home on leave;

I'd hide under the kitchen table

from their big voices and their talk about guns.

No one ever asked how I was doing.

Years later, after Mom died,

I was suppose to wash their socks

and make chicken gravy just like she did.

A house full of brothers, turned to soldiers,

turned to blue airmail letters in the mailbox.

I LISTENED to loud music and danced

into my teenage years,

always afraid of something I couldn't name.

AFTERMATH

There was a place behind the barn
they would occasionally sneak a smoke or two,
matches rolled in their cotton T-shirt sleeves;
they wanted to be like the older boys.
They wanted to bathe on Saturday nights
and put on cologne and go girlin' in town.
The house always smelled like hair tonic then,
like stiff new Levis and saddle soap.
Everyone smiled on Saturday nights.

THE WEEK of the Fourth of July
the older boys talked about the races at Clear Lake
on Saturday and the rodeo on Sunday
and the beer they were going to drink all weekend.

And since Terry and Tim didn't drive

and their brothers had no interest in taking them,

they swore about it out behind the barn

between shallow drags from Papa's Winstons.

WHEN SATURDAY CAME, Terry and Tim

took the string of Black Cats out behind the straw stacks

and divvied up ammo for the war.

They talked tough battle talk

and cussed and pointed at the house

as if it were enemy lines.

When the older boys piled into the green Chevy

and the '57 Ford pick-up headed for Clear Lake,

the two soldiers lit their punks

and the firecrackers came to life.

Three or four sets went off

as the cars reached the road

and skidded to a stop on the loose gravel.

The older boys swore out the windows,

but then drove away,

and the two young ones

felt the battle had happened

all too fast. They sat

with the rest of their ammo

and no war to go to, sat not talking

until a crackling sound like electricity

and the smell of late autumn curled

around from the other side of the stack.

Horses in the corral snorted with fear.

Not long after, the fire truck from town

howled into the yard,

filling the air with too much noise.

OUT BEHIND THE BARN, as sweat mixed in

with the summer dust on their necks,

Terry told Tim to ignore the calls

from the house. He knew

there was no where to go but jail;

they were in no hurry.

Finally, tired and anxious

and ready to give themselves up,

the boys walked around the barn

into the full sunshine.

Tim saw the path of the fire first,

the straw stack, the corral fence

down to the windmill,

and a patch of dry grass between,

now all black and charred

like ditches at spring burning.

THE OLD FIRE truck had gone.

No one was around.

Stepping into the house, ready for the belt

and what was to come,

they met their mother with warm cookies

and two cold glasses of milk.

"I saw you walking in.

Take off those filthy boots

and wash your hands, both of you."

ALMOST SMILING, unable to contain

a mother's joy at all that remained,

she set the glasses on the kitchen table,

wiped her hands on her cotton apron,

and left the room.

TELEGRAM

In a glass box, inside a glass box

in the iced city of Moscow,

he sits before a tool box

with a yellow telegram in his hand.

The bare bulb overhead hums,

gives off a bluish light,

sounds like bees trapped

between the window and the screen.

"It's my mother" he says

to no one at all, to the wall,

to the dress uniform

his fingers brush across lightly

as he packs his bags for home.

UNCLE EDDIE BUILDS A HOUSE

In the kitchen of his square apartment,
night after night after each day
at vocational school, he built the house
for my younger sisters' dolls. Used his tools
and training to build scalloped awnings,
wooden shutters, a curved staircase.
It seemed the miniature rooms had windows
that looked out onto Switzerland,
onto white-capped mountains and safe cows
with bells around their necks, onto a world
far away from the postage-stamp-sized shingles
he glued into place one by one.
He rebuilt his life with tweezers and wood glue.

. . .

HE REMEMBERED Vietnam where nothing small

survived.

"When Mom died I came home to help out

and my buddies . . . well they died

without me. Shit, that's hard to live with. I

started slipping. Left my car stranded

on the county road eight miles from home

and never looked back.

Called your mom from a bus depot in Marshall

and didn't know how the hell I'd gotten there.

She drove across the prairie, picked me up

and took me home to live with you. Remember?

I rode a bike around the lake to town

and cleaned chickens at the soup factory,

pumped gas on weekends for extra money

for carpenter school. I figured

I'd always been good with my hands."

THE NEXT TIME we visited Ed,

the dollhouse was gone.

"Got behind on my rent," he said. "Landlord

let himself in and stepped on it . . .

broke the thing to bits. Threw it against the

goddamn kitchen wall."

Something like anger took over then;

anger, crowded with confusion,

grabbed his voice

and turned it into something else.

"I'm sorry, little darlings," he said

"that your dollies

won't have a nice home."

ROBERT M. IN THE DOORWAY

It isn't what he says about the service
but what he doesn't say about that night
when Hank McCarty bent over the toolbox
and the light bulb did that thing
around his head
before the grenade went off.

> You got to understand the smell of a campfire --
> it never leaves no matter where you go
> or what jungle you remember he is always with
> you that friend on the nicest day of spring when
> you take a deep breath and then hear him joking
> before it is all over it is never over you are never
> alone again.

There are too many bombs
ready to detonate inside him,

too many arms lying limp

near the pillars of war.

I cannot ask him anything.

He feels it all again like an earthquake

with each question.

II. AIRMAIL

VOICES, A COLLAGE

1965-1966

Dear Mom and Dad,
I received your most welcomed letter today.

Let's see . . . Liberia. Abidjan, Ivory Coast.

La Gos, Nigeria. Beirut, Lebanon. Tehran, Iran.

I've been busy.

Seems I don't get unpacked and I'm leaving again.

   9 October. Yes. I've reenlisted.

Six more years in the good old United States Navy.

I've given it a tremendous amount of thought;

I have so much time to think here . . .

I guess the service has as much to offer me
as anything else.

    I enjoy traveling and seeing things.

    16 October. Dear Mom, Dad and Kids,

I got my orders to Vietnam but there is some confusion.
I'll keep you posted.
Your Son, Bobby
Sorry to hear Eddie got orders to Vietnam;
he is not in the best racket. He wrote to me,
told me he volunteered for it. I'm not impressed.
I know he's torn up over a girl.
Love does funny things.
We must pray for his safety now.

    Dear Folks,

Glad to hear Bob didn't have to go to Vietnam
yet and that Bill's back. Let me know
what you hear from Ed, will you?
Did that last snowstorm hit you people or not?
Just what will he be doing over there, Mom?
Will he be right in the field or what?
Write when you have time.

Clem and family

1967

DEAREST FAMILY, I've been here at Camp Alpha
three days and haven't shipped out or heard
any orders heard anything about where
I'm going yet. Tell Sandy, if you see her,
I'll write soon as I get orders.

    24 January.

This damn place is getting on my nerves.
It sure as hell is hot here.
Today's a scorcher--
my nose is redder than a tomato.
How is the farm work coming, Dad?
Is it keeping you busy?
As of today, I've been here a week.
It's hot as hell. I'm not kidding. I wish
I was back there. I wish
I was home.

    Dear Sis,

Have you heard from Eddie

since he arrived in Vietnam?

Have you heard from Eddie

since he got over there?

What's Eddie's address, Mom? What do you

hear from him? Where is Bill now?

Do you know his orders? Say, do you know

where Bob is these days?

I haven't heard from him.

Got a letter from Clem. Sounds like

he's got a nice place out there.

I'd like to visit them sometime.

    Dear Sis,

Have you heard anything from Bob?

    Hello Everyone.

I'm learning something new every day.

To see what these Vietnamese people

are going through is something else.

You can't imagine it, Ma. I wouldn't have

believed it if I didn't see it

with my own two eyes.

I don't believe you'll ever hear me complain

about anything again.

Do you know where Bill is now?

Have you heard?

February, 1967, Bearcat.

I am just outside of Long Binh,
a bunch of old tents and dusty as all get out.
Walking to chow, my boots sink into about
three inches of fine red dirt. Even finer
than the dirt road on the farm after tractors
and trailers grind it down like flour.
We sleep in a big tent with fine screens
for windows and every time a helicopter
takes off, red dust sifts in so you can't see
across the room. In the morning, I wake up,
about a pound of dust on my blankets. I mean it.
I have to shake myself off like an old dog.
That's what a guy gets for volunteering
for his country.
A hardship tour, they call it,
but they ain't talking about the dust.
I finally saw the inside of a gunship.
A slow flying whale of a helicopter.
Went up to Saigon and then Long Binh.

We received fire from Charlie and returned it,

but nothing serious. Just scored me a little,

being up the air, 2,100 points

and maybe needing to come down

amongst a bunch of Charlies,

but we didn't take any lead

and I was happy about that.

Not much else to report.

We work 5:30 AM to 5:30 PM

then see a movie every night.

Drive-in style without the cars.

We watch it in our T-shirts and skivvy drawers.

Then we take our nightly showers

and crawl into a dusty bed.

I'll try to get some pictures of this place.

You can't imagine the dust.

    Hello, Sis.

I guess it's too early to talk

about coming home. Two years and two months

and I'll have five years in. That should do

for my service to the good old U.S.A..

Sis, I want to get married soon. Settle down.

Find a decent job. I realize it takes two,

but I think I have her almost convinced.

Maybe one or two more leaves and maybe

everything will be straightened out.

I've always wanted to drive across the country.

Do a little fishing, stay someplace a while

if it looks nice, but I guess

dreaming can be dangerous.

This place is about as good as any over here.

We haven't been mortared for quite awhile.

We're expecting an Aviation Unit from the States

and then it's pretty much a guarantee

when we get our choppers we'll get fire.

I only hope they don't get too close.

I never did like hot lead.

Remember the time, Colleen, you got sunburned

so bad fishing at the lake?

My neck and arms are burned as bad,

if not worse. Now it feels like the heat

of the jungle is coming out from my insides, too.

You can imagine how I feel.

Kiss the kids for me, you know,

on their foreheads, right above the eyebrows.

Write me a letter; remember me in your prayers.

Your red-headed Eddie

    Good news. I got some good news

and can't wait to let you hear it. I'm feeling good

writing this letter, telling you hello,

telling you this morning in formation

the company commander called me out.

Then the Battalion Commander

presented me with my promotion. It was early;

it was a proud moment for me.

Now for the bad news.

We've been on a thirty-six hour alert.

Old Charlie is supposed to mortar us.

We've got sixteen Chinook Choppers in

and he's trying for them.

He blew up the road between here and Saigon

Sunday morning. Blew it up in four different

places. Don't worry,

don't worry. I'll be just fine. Just write to me.

All of you write when you can.

P.S. Tell the little boys I said "hi"

and I wish them luck fishing.

If they need any advice on how to catch a fish,
you just let me know.

    Mom. Don't worry too much about me

all the time. I told you I'd let you know
everything that went on
over here. I'd let you know first. I said so.
Last night we got four or five rounds
of mortar fire on the port. Across the port
from us. Four men wounded. It went off
at one o'clock and we stayed up until
three-thirty. Everything was so quiet after that.
There's nothing to worry about, Mom.
I will keep you up-to-date, I promise.

    Do me a favor Mom and don't let this

kind of news worry you so much.
I'm not anywhere near any real fighting.
True they harass us, but not enough
to do any real damage. Please don't worry
so much about me. Please don't worry.
I'm all right. There's no real damage. Nothing to
worry about. Nothing. I promise. Don't worry.

    Mom. I am sorry about the money

that you had to send to the IRS.

The way I had it figured was I would get some

back. I know I've caused you and Dad

undue hardship since I've been in the Army.

I'm sorry.

    Received your letter and must say

I'm sorry that you broke your ankle, Mom.

Does it hurt a lot? Is the cast hot?

I guess the Smiths are cut out for hard luck.

    Received the package of razor blades

and Noxzema yesterday and want to thank you

for it. Thank you, very much.

I'm always sunburned.

It's hot as hell here.

    I've been here four months and ten days.

Am going down hill and getting shorter

with every passing second.

Can't wait until I get orders back to the world.

Can't say what your letters mean every week,

Mom. And the kids. Tell them I love their letters.

Tell the kids I love them. Your loving son #5, Ed

    The mail just came in so I'll check it.

Nothing. So I'll just say "Sin Loe." So long.
P.S. There's a picture of Sandy in the cubbyhole
of my car. Would you please send it along
with the stand or that little brown case.
Thanks. Thanks a lot.

    28 May. Well, here we are.

Another week gone by and it's Sunday
in Moscow. Spring refuses to arrive.
I suppose you have the crops in Dad.
I sit awake some nights and think about
driving a tractor down
straight rows of growing green.
Remember the summer of '65 when I was home
and Chuck and I did a little haying?
I lie awake now and imagine I hear
the cry of the crickets.
It helps me fall asleep.
It was very good to hear from you
and I hope to again, soon. All my love, Bobby

1968-1969

    Dear Dad,

DEAR DAD AND KIDS,

I find it hard to write letters, harder still

not to write them. You know my mail

is all I have over here.

It's a blue day. Forgive me.

The ocean seems worlds away

and you all, even further.

    Hey, kids. You all help your Daddy now.

He needs you around. He needs

all the help you can give him. I wish

I were home and could help you too.

    Dear Dad. Glad to see Eddie got work.

I know we've never been real close

but I was surprised at his indifference to me

when I was home for Mom's funeral.

I know the transition from military

to civilian life must be a drastic change.

And these difficult circumstances.

You see, the things which you people deem

necessities mean very little to a service man.

And the warm safety of home is hard to believe

in the middle of a dark night.

    Who does Delores confide in anyway

now that Mom's gone? So young

to have so much responsibility.

Bless her, she's doing a terrific job.

And little Tim.

Missing all those years. It's hard to think about.

    How is it going Dad?

Have you heard from Bob

since he got back to Moscow? Did Clem's car

make the trip back to Oregon okay?

How is Ed doing?

Is he working? Is he going to go to school?

Has he checked into the GI Bill?

How has Judy been since Mom's death?

I know she was all broke up; she

can be a handful. I hope it works out okay.

No word from you folks this week or last.

I presume it got held up somewhere.
It often does.

You know, although it's been six months

since Mom passed away, I still look
for her weekly letters. I don't know
how many times I've read her last letter to me.
She praised all of her kids
for making such a nice Mother's Day for her.
She was worried because Colleen
wouldn't see a doctor, Chuckie hadn't written
and Eddie was "over there."
Hell, how did she keep up the pace she did
and still manage to smile?
I think that group home is a good idea for Judy.
God knows Mom was good with her
but it hasn't been easy, I know.
I'm sure Judy will be happier around other
people. It must be lonely in that house
while the kids are at school.
I'd like to see her find a little happiness.

Doesn't Delores' personality strike you

as really something? You know when I was

home I had the opportunity to observe her

and I found that she was so well-adjusted.

It amazed me that someone of her age

could cope with the tragedy of Mom's death

and then take care of a house full of men.

    3 February.

We lost another man last week.

(For reasons I will not explain.)

Now it's just the Chief and me left.

I'd sure like to be able to talk to Eddie.

Sorry to hear about the nightmares

and the struggle he's having.

    Quang Tri, Vietnam.

I'm sure tired of this place

and I still have a while left to do over here.

The dampness and the humidity get real hard

to live with. The big B-52's hit just north of here

all day long and that is an experience in itself.

    What do you folks hear from Bill?

When will he be coming home again?

Does he know for sure where he will be going
next? How is Eddie doing? Is he settling down?
I'm afraid I was on his back too much
when I was home on leave.

    Now that my weekly letter

is no longer arriving, it is my constant worry
as to how Dad and the kids are getting along.
I spent one day in Washington
then on to McGuire Air Force Base in
New Jersey, then to Frankfurt, Germany where
I spent four days awaiting transportation
to Moscow. On to Stockholm, Sweden,
Copenhagen, Denmark and into Moscow, USSR,
arriving at ten o'clock on the first day of July.
Is Eddie's discharge final?
Colleen, next time you get up home, will you
check and see if those folks have sent out my photos?
I had three rolls of color film in the City Drug.
I'm sure they're ready and both
Chuck and Ed promised to mail them out.
It would help to have some new photographs
of you all. I don't check for mail anymore.

If I have any, fine.

If not, I'm not as disappointed.

I called home last Sunday and spoke with Dee

and Chuck. We talked for eleven minutes.

It cost sixty-four dollars. I wish Dad had been

home. What do you think of the little ponies

I bought Tim? Is he riding them much?

I used to live for the times I came home

and we'd put on the coffee pot and talk all night.

I'm so thankful I had that leave at Easter

and saw Mom. When I got back here,

her last letter had just arrived telling me

about her broken ankle. Thanking me for

her Mother's Day gift and telling me

what a wonderful son I was. Hell.

Please check on the pictures, Sis.

I've enclosed a check.

If you could take Tim, Terry and Dee

to the city and get them what they need

for school. It isn't much, but it's the best I can do

right now. I have always enjoyed my work,

but leaving home after mother's funeral

and telling the little ones good-bye was hell.

I dreamed last night I was coming home. I was

driving that red Buick convertible

and stopped to eat at a restaurant on the way.

The table was set with a linen cloth

and all this beautiful china. I sat and ate steak

and corn on the cob

and drank glass after glass of ice cold milk.

I knew you all were expecting me,

but I took my time and enjoyed the lovely meal.

And no one was

standing there breathing down my neck.

No one numbering my days.

1970-1979

Dear Dad,

AS OF TOMORROW morning

I will have twelve days to go before I jump

on that airplane to head home for Christmas.

Doris says when the kids talk about

their dad coming home they get so excited

sparks start to fly. I hate to be separated,

but I'm still a very lucky man

to have a wife and four wonderful children
to go home to. Just six months left to go
before I retire. Oh, the wages are good now
and it would be nice to stick around
and pick up another stripe,
but we don't want any more family separations.
Love, Bill

    Well, Dad, how are things at home?

Have any of the boys been home yet?
What do you hear from Clem?
Is Terry working or not?
I sure wanted an opportunity to talk with him
before he joins the service.
Is he planning on going before fall?

    Thailand.

Well, how about a letter
from the boys? It only takes five minutes
to write a short letter and I would
sure appreciate it. I may get sent to Bangkok or
Utapau for seven to ten days of schooling
on the equipment. I'll probably learn something.
I work three day shifts of eleven hours,

then three night shifts of thirteen hours apiece,

then have seventy-two hours off.

Love, Terry

How's my car running, Charlie?

Bill says Bob is trying to get out of China

next month and put in for a thirty day leave.

Hope he makes it. He sure hasn't had

a long leave at home for a long time.

Keep catching those fish 'cause

you are going to need the practice

when I get home.

We'll run up into Minnesota or Canada

for a full week when I get home.

How does that sound Dad?

We'll catch some fish

and have a really good time.

Hell, it ain't very far up there and it'll be a great

trip. So plan on it, okay?

If no one else wants to go,

you and me will, okay?

We've done lots of good fishing together over

the years Dad and I want to, I plan to,

do some more. Love your #6 Son

I'm going to close and get some sleep but will you answer these questions in your next letter, please?

    1. How much money do I have in my savings account?
I show two hundred and thirty-five dollars.
    2. How much is in my checking account?
    3. Please send me my bank statements, okay?

I'm nearly one-third of the way through my year here. What has been happening back there? Anything going on or is it about the same?

Love your #6 Son

Are you guys able to get heating fuel okay up there? Sure wouldn't want you to run out in the middle of a blizzard.

    I got a good long letter from Bob.

Sent one off to his D.C. address the other day as I had heard he was in Austria. Got a nice long letter from Doris. She says they love Montana and are anxiously waiting to have Bill home for Christmas.

    I can hardly wait to hit the States again and for November 1975 to roll around.

    Well Sis, I received your package

yesterday and we proceeded to devour
most of its contents. Everyone loved
your cookies. I even saved a few
for tomorrow. I sure thank you.
We got a charge out of reading
what was on those candy hearts also.

    Don't know what else I'd like to do,

but am getting out of this service shit for sure.
Just one hundred and thirty-three days left.

    Hello, Pa. How are things

at my wonderful home in South Dakota?

    10 March, 1974

Dar Es Salaam, Tanzani, Jidda, Saudi Arabia,
Addis Ababa, Ethiopia, Nairobi, Kenya.
I haven't received any mail for five weeks.
Don't know what's going on.

    Tell Charlie to get off his ass

and drop me a line, will you? God damn,
it only takes ten minutes; I can't believe he could
sit in that house all winter

and not even drop a guy a line.

Tell the boys

I want to see them plant the potatoes

like we talked about.

I thoroughly enjoyed my long leave at home

last fall. I treasure the memory of it.

Particularly the time I was able to spend

with you, Dad, and little Tim.

You got to admit,

we did shoot some pheasants, huh?

    I am in receipt of your letter of 18 March

and was very glad to hear from you.

    Say Dad, I've written to Delores

but haven't heard from her yet.

When is her wedding date?

I don't suppose I'll be able to make it home,

but if things work out I just may be in the States

about that time. Tell her to let me know,

will you? I sure would like to see that!

    I received a real nice long letter from Bill

last week. I sure enjoy getting mail.

This can be a damned lonesome old life, Pa.

I have written to Delores but haven't heard from her yet. When is her wedding date?

It looks like we are going to Nairobi, Kenya next. Say, would you tell Delores to drop me a line.
I might be able to get home for the wedding but as of yet I don't know the date.

I suppose you folks are enjoying some real nice weather by now, huh?
I am going to try and get home this summer. Think you can round up an extra fishing pole?

Tell Tim to drop me a line sometime, okay? Say Dad, I'll be damned if I can get a wedding date from you people.
I am trying to schedule myself to where I can make it home. It's possible if I KNOW WHEN!

I suppose by now you have heard from the boys, haven't you Dad?

If you have, then I would like addresses for Bill, Clem, and Tim. Is Charlie working yet? If so, where?

How is the spring treating you?

Has my mare had a colt yet? When she does, please get a picture of it will you?

How is the fishing Dad?

BUCHAREST, Romania. What kind of summer are you having? Hot? Wet? How do the crops look? Did Charlie get any hay from Richard or not? Please remember to get about fifty bushels of oats
when Richard combines will you?

Has Dusty had her colt yet?

If she has, I would sure like some photos of it as soon as possible.

I hear Ed reenlisted. He told me
he needs a sergeant to keep him in line. Well, good for him, I say. It can be a tough life sometimes, but I think Ed will do all right by it.

21 July, 1975

Your loving son #5, Ed

P.S. What are they saying in the news back home
about Korea now? If anything, don't worry Dad.
Okay?

    Still haven't heard from Bob.

Where in the hell is he located now?

    Glad to hear Chuck finally got a job.

Tell him he owes me a letter.

    How is fishing up at Lake Poinsett?

Clear Lake? What's the weather been at home?
Have you had much rain or is it hot as hell?
Where are you fishing? At the creek
under the bridge? Out in the pasture?
Have they been hitting pretty good or just hit
and miss? Hope to see you
in eighty-eight to ninety-four days.

    Thanks a million for your last letter, Dad.

Sorry I haven't gotten you a suit made yet.
I know I promised to get one before now,

but I guess I never could keep my word
about anything.

    1976, January.

We are finished here and will be going
to Algiers, Algeria, North Africa late this week.
Should be a good job.
Is Charlie working construction?
How does he like it?
What do you hear from the boys? Tim and Ed?
Terry should be damned near finished now, isn't he?
Is Charlie still unemployed or what?
Did Delores have her baby? Is everything okay?
How about my little Dusty mare? A colt?
No colt? Did I get back a tax dividend?
If so, did you put it in my checking account?
I sure would like to hear from you folks.
Still don't have Bill's new address
so I can't write to him.

    How the hell is everything in Dakota?

Well Dad, this Egypt is a hot, damn place.
You probably won't believe it
but I am sure getting tired of traveling.

Hell, I hardly get unpacked sometimes.

(I have had the dysentery ever since I got here.)

    Dad, I'm sorry I haven't written more,

but you know how one day blurs into another.

I am still in Alexandria, Egypt.

I was supposed to leave here

over two weeks ago,

but we got roped into providing security

for the Kissinger peace talks,

and it's just been run, run, run.

He's leaving soon, so maybe things

will settle down.

I'm slated to got to Algiers and expect to move

any day now. I may not show it,

but I love you Dad!

And I want you to know that.

Pray for peace throughout the world!

    I'll finish here around April first

and if the boss will let me I want to take

three or four days to go through Germany

on my way home and see Tim.

The mail is screwed up again.

They were routing through Athens and
switched to Paris.
I guess most of the embassy's Christmas mail
is still sitting in Athens.

    What's the weather been like Dad?

Has it been cold? Done any ice fishing?
Is Terry going to go to school?
I suppose he's content
to draw some rocking chair money for awhile.
Lord knows he's got it coming.
I'll drop Tim and Ed a line.
Take care, okay?

    Paris, France. 1800 hours.

Well, Pa. I finished in Algiers and would have
been visiting little brother Tim next week
in Germany, but got a message this morning.
Seems they had a bad find in the embassy
in Libreville, Gabon, West Africa.
I'm leaving Paris at ten tonight for Gabon,
so I'll let you know how it goes, okay?
As always, you son, Bob

Istanbul, Turkey. As you can see

I finally got out of Africa. How is Charlie doing?

Is he working yet?

What do you hear from Ed?

When is he going to be back in the States?

How is little Tim doing?

I can't tell you how damned excited I am

about returning to the States and being

stationed in California. Oh, I've enjoyed my

travels and it has damned sure been educational.

Now I want to see America.

SIGNING OFF FOR TONIGHT.

Good Night, Pa.

Love Always,

Love,

See You at Christmas in eight months and five days,

With All My Love,

Your Son,

  As Always,

Better get some shut-eye.

  Love you always, your loving son,

Write Soon.

  If anything, don't worry Dad,

With all my love,

  As always, your son,

God Bless You Always,

  Love,

Love,

  See you soon,

Wish I was home.

III. SURVIVING

FIRST BORN

You have to understand
I was the oldest of ten and all those brothers

and after she died, I felt, I don't know,

like I'd been an extension of her,

a shadow maybe and now

I was supposed to be a whole person.

I tried to write to the boys overseas

every week, tried to help the young ones

without stepping on toes, not trying

to take Mom's place, I'd never do that.

Good memories of growing up?

That's a hard one. It was always the boys.

. . .

Yes, I wrote to all of them

whenever I could, raised my own family

and don't regret a thing. I wasn't a boy,

that was my sin and I was the one

made her get married in the first place.

She told me that again and again.

It was my fault and look what it got her.

"My little mother" she told an aunt once,

"helps out so much" but she never said it

to my face. I overheard from the pantry,

felt such pride it grew like a flower inside me,

kept me writing letters and soothing brows

for the rest of my life. Kept me whispering into the ear

of the brother who needed it most

"I love you; you are worthwhile;

hang in there."

BROTHER ON LEAVE

Ah hell, he got a little drunk and decided
he was going to beat some patriotism into me.
Two or three fists to the face and stomach

and I went underwater,

grabbing and scratching like a polecat in a gunny sack.

God, I hated him then.

Hated the smell of whiskey and beer, the blaring

body counts on NBC every night.

Hated the letters we got in the mailbox

for what my brothers couldn't say,

hated the blank sheet of paper

when I tried to write back. I had just got home

from basketball practice,

he shoved my duffel bag off the table

and it accidentally spilled his beer.

I know now it wasn't me he was fighting,

but I wasn't ready to enlist in any damn war.

I was a kid,

a five-foot-ten guard

who scored sixteen points against Preston

on Friday night. Sixteen points,

five rebounds and four assists.

LOVE, COLLEEN

I know, and yet.
It is difficult to write these words,
to send these negative thoughts
across so many ocean miles,
and after all you've been through.
But I worry.
He is getting close to draft age and

> *I am glad to hear Terry is doing okay, Sis.*
> *Yes, I understand how you feel*
> *in reference to his joining the service*
> *now in the middle of this.*

has had to grow up so fast. Vietnam
is too close and I don't see any other scenario.

> *I want him to get an education*

about as much as I want anything.
I know he knows it, but
I also know how a young man feels
when he reaches draft age.

He thinks about his older brothers,

doesn't say much but when he does he

says a lot in a little. I've tried to talk to him.

He's proud. Puts a fence up when words about

war enter into the kitchen conversation.

I like to rationalize and think that maybe
his five brothers have bought him
his college time. And as far as feeling guilty,
he certainly has no reason to.

I sit here with my own son nearing draft age

and wish this damn war would go away,

wish I could put my hands out and touch you

across the table, ask you

if you'd like more coffee,

tell you about the ordinariness of my day.

PICKING ROCK

Two weeks out of high school, too much
to figure out, stacking rocks
on the fence line, helping Dad clear the field
and *what about a job?*
How am I going to make it?
It'll work out, son. Something will come up.
Until then you can help me.
At school they'd say: *Go to college, Terry.*
You're smart. Get a degree.
The boys down the road go to college.
They got money. We got the military.
I got a lump in my throat.
Dad always wanted one of us to stay and farm
with him, but that crystal ball was too small.

Maybe Junior College? Draft number 69.

I get crap from my brothers about choosing

the Air Force, but I can live with that.

I don't want to be a foot soldier

and get shot at and sunburned in Vietnam.

I'm a Smith boy. I love my country,

but I don't want to

die.

SMOKE ON THE WATER

"Hell, it ain't like you're going into the military kid,

it's just the Air Force,"

says one brother the night before he takes off,

before he flies over South Dakota fields

and strains hard to see what's corn,

what's wheat.

Before he flies into a haze that lasts and lasts.

He breathes deep and holds it.

Closes his eyes to the ocean between this place

and the world that he knows.

The one that will be smaller and less brilliant

when he goes back.

The jukebox plays one song in English.

Deep Purple's "Smoke on the Water."

He goes to sleep a teenager and wakes up

in Thailand in a dead-end communications

center with nothing to do. If it ain't broke,

don't fix it. If it is, haul ass boy,

the U. S. Armed Forces are depending on you!

Outside an old Thai man sells gun-shy dope.

Two joints for a quarter.

This ain't South Dakota. This ain't clear straight-

shooting man on man take it to the hoop stuff.

Somebody messed with the rules

and four years is a long time.

He is connecting the dots,

he is the sixth of seven sons

who enlisted, who all served their time.

I'M TALLER, TIM

You try to skip over being eleven
when I am ten and taller and everyone
points it out.
We play soldiers out in the arthritic trees,
shoot bee-bee guns at juice cans and sparrows,
plan flank attacks behind the chicken coop.
Later, you leave high school early
and do what you've learned all your life.

YOU JOIN the Army and walk proud.
I help you fill out the forms
at the dining room table,
then we play some Buck Euchre.

Someone takes a photograph.

I am sixteen and uneasy.

Keep your head down, I want to say.

Grandma is gone, but I'll write to you.

I'll never stop writing to you.

CHRISTMAS LEAVE

There were times when saying good-bye
was more than any of us could take.
I usually flew out when the kids were asleep,
but this one time it was an afternoon flight
and they came along to the airport.
Christmas, 1973.
Almost halfway through my last tour.
It was rough on all of us, trying to act like
everything was going to be . . .
Christmas Eve I played on the floor with my son
and his new train.
We went for long walks; Doris and I pulled
the three little ones on sleds all over town.
Early evening, when the snow

drifted down in the circle of a street light,

I closed my eyes to memorize the sight,

the smell of a cold Montana night,

the weight of my children

on the sled behind me.

One year and forty days to go.

WRITE SOON

In the gap between letters,
Egypt gets so damned hot,
I long for Oak Lake

and the sound of wind in the cottonwoods.

The people here speak softly

and never smile.

It is the children

who point at my strawberry-blond hair

and sunburned face,

point and smile

and run off into dark places

between buildings.

Run off and play their games,

the games of children,

and I feel their absence

against my burning skin.

FUNNY MONEY

Finally, really going somewhere!
Lampang, Thailand.
How much money is that?
I don't know, but I got some change back.
Stay close to camp. Gamble when you're drunk.
Funny money. Hurry up and wait. The world
goes slower over here. Play some basketball.
Shoot hoops for money. Six guys on your team
against twenty MP's.
You shake 'em up! It feels good to be a winner.
It feels good to hold a basketball again,
like home in your hands, like the corn crib court
after chores, shoot under a bare light bulb

until it's only you and the ball,

until twenty-five free throws in a row go down.

Until you make a bet with yourself and win.

DECISIONS

I'm over the half-way mark today.
Six months exactly
and I'm looking forward to getting out
to getting out of here.
I've saved one thousand and fifty dollars
so far. I figure
when I reach the fifteen hundred mark
I'll start buying junk buying junk
and sending it home.
They have beautiful jade jewelry the
jewelry is beautiful here.
I've saved one thousand and fifty I can't wait
can't wait to get out of here.

. . .

I'VE HAD a notion to go into the Marines

when I'm done with this enlistment a notion

but I know most of the guys

who go into the Marines

are either trying to prove something

to themselves or to somebody else and besides

I ain't trying to prove nothing to nobody.

I just want out of the Air Force I

just want to do what I want

I wish I knew what that was.

I do know I want to hunt and fish

and laugh a lot I've

thought that far I've thought about laughing.

They say the guys that talk most

about getting out are the ones that re-enlist.

They say that but don't worry it's not true

in my case. Don't think that it's true.

I might stay in though. A guy never knows.

Anyway I have twenty-one months to decide

what I'm going to do twenty-one months

before I need to sign need to sign

on another line

so I figure no sweat for now.

SURVIVOR

You made it past cancer,
past the goblins in your veins,
the sawdust in your mouth
day after struggling day,
to sit in a boat on the Kenai River
and pray to shadows of salmon
under a clouded sky.
Thanking the rain for the feel of it,
for the cold fingers on your face,
you set the hook into your life

AND GRASP the pole with both hands,

the treacherous shore still in sight,

death but a memory playing the line.

INTERVIEW WITH DEE

She answers questions dutifully.
One hand touches her lips
before she speaks,
comes back to her mouth again
and again, as if it is necessary
to release each word with her fingertips.
Her other hand, fisted in near her waist,
holds back everything else.
For her, the family history centers
on the death of her mother
when she was only twelve.
She can tell me about brothers she hardly knew
cleaning guns at the kitchen table at night,

about the phone call from the Pentagon

on Christmas Eve, and the brother

who left for Cambodia one hour later,

about the secrets he couldn't share.

She can tell story after story about brothers

on leave and battlefield nightmares

and the longing and the absence

which was always a part of her life.

Instead, she tells me

about learning to identify trees.

How her dad used to stop the car

and pull leaves from the branches and tell her

the names of each one.

He said one day she'd be happy she knew

an oak from a black walnut.

Her skin holds in the building pressure

of sorrow, the tears that fill every pore

of her body, the tears that seem

to have always been there.

All of her brothers came home,

but she needed to talk to a woman.

She was the second youngest of ten and a girl.

. . .

There was no one to say yes, I understand

and yes, this is natural

and yes, yes, you are a woman now.

SILK DRAGONS

We sit in the kitchen,
fluorescent hum
of midnight between us,
and talk around years of nameless sex,
screen doors left open and banging.
Jokes like slipcovers over everything.
I want to know why, but do not ask.
He wants to tell me.
He does not.

FAMILY BLAMES THE WAR.

He came back a little less married.

Found out the first time

he looked at her, knew it was all over,

knew it wasn't.

I never knew her.

And something about chemicals in that war.

Rashes. I don't know; I was a child.

I remember a Korean jacket

covered with silk dragons,

their wild tails curling.

SMELL OF HORSE hair and sweat.

The coffee boils to nothing.

"But you have your life," I say.

"Give it a rest, Kate.

This ol' cowboy's dust.

I'm walking to Kansas City."

And he does as we sit there,

all night talking, together,

in the cream and sugar kitchen

and welcome him home.

CLEM

I don't want to chase you
into the Oregon hills,
use you up for the sake of this damn story,
but remembering is what I do.
We dug clams that summer and said little.
You handed me the shovel
and told me to be quick.
I was a teenager swallowed
by my own insecurities,
with an uncle I knew only from pictures
and that one week after Grandma's funeral,
when you all painted the house.
Far from the prairie that summer,
you showed me driftwood--

the power of wind, water and salt

and I knew I had visited

my first foreign country.

Years later, I asked you about those years

in uniform, sent a letter to an address

I'd never seen.

I didn't hear back, but then, at Charlie's funeral,

you arrived in a red pickup in time for taps.

Your brothers told me you served on a ship.

Peeled potatoes and kept to yourself.

You have always kept to yourself.

They told me everything they knew,

which was nothing, in the end,

and I guessed the rest, which was even less.

I will not invent you now

for the sake of this family portrait,

but I will say I see your slanted shoulder

standing next to all your brothers

but one, a baseball cap shading your eyes

from more than the sadness of the sun.

DON'T FORGET THE WOMEN

"Don't forget the women,"
you said the last time
I saw you alive.
"That war, any war, shit,
they never get any credit.
You write that in your poem.
Vietnam. Two hundred and sixty-five thousand women,
ten thousand in country.
Did you hear about that monument?
Well then, you write that down, Kate.
You start with the young nurse
who saved one scared kid;
put her on her knees,

like an angel, like a true bit of honor,

the kid cradled there in her arms; you

make her the only one that kid sees

when he decides whether to live or die.

Those women. You understand?"

THE YOUNGEST ONE

He grew into himself
at the tail-end of Vietnam. Enlisted
at seventeen to stay out of small-town trouble.
Six brothers served before him. Five
in Southeast Asia. The country believed
it was all over but no one in the military
ever did. Even so, he ended up in Germany,
spent his days off in beer gardens
as American planes practiced
their cat and mouse over the city.
As homesick as the rest of them,
Tim did not dream the splintered torture
of a war zone, nor did he get weekly letters
of love. He had been fighting his own war

since the fifth grade.

When you are a child and your mother dies,

an invisible glass wall goes up around you.

You learn to walk without breaking it;

you learn to live in the cylinder

and grow good at it. You learn to talk

whatever language people are speaking,

but all of your life your mind talks to you

in a language only you understand.

LOST RECORDS

It is in the kitchen, always the kitchen,
chrome and Formica dull now,
cupboards with shallow grooves
under the handles
where hands have reached for coffee cups
for over fifty years. He relaxes after a few beers
and hours of walking the corn fields
for pheasants.

> Did I ever tell you?
> I was in Cambodia when no one
> was in Cambodia, got sick --
> airvac'd out and almost bled to death.
> Now that I'm retired,
> this story seems less and less real
> every time I tell it.
> But this ain't no shit.

*Cynical? You bet your ass.
I was up for a Mustang promotion.
That's the top of the line in the Sea Bees
of the U. S. Navy, so I'm filling out all the forms.
Medevaced out of Cambodia
to the Army's 5th Field Hospital.
Bangkok, Thailand.
First diagnosis: Bleeding Ulcer.
It turns out it was a parasite
chewing up my intestines and the wall
of my stomach. A parasite
I'd gotten years earlier
while stationed in the Tropics.
So I'm writing this medical history out
on their forms
and this young officer says Petty Officer Smith,
a little heavy on the "t's" like Webster's
definition of petty, right? Well, he says,
Petty Officer Smith, there's a mistake here.
No American Military Personnel
was in Cambodia in October of 1970.
Yes, sir. I know that sir, I said.
But, you see, I was.
Check my records, my medical history,
it should all be there.
So he says, our records show
you were never in Cambodia.
And it pussy-assed on and on like that
from one asshole in uniform on up the ladder.
Six weeks, six months, a year. Fill out the forms
again sailor, and I did. Finally, it ends up
on the desk of the Admiral in charge
of the Bureau of Medicine, and I still
put down the facts on the form, and they see*

*I deserve this promotion and
I can't be of any use this way
so they promote my ass and shut me up.
Somewhere between war and peace
my records were misplaced.
Mistaken. Misinformed.
Well Kath, I'm here to say, in 1970,
you wrote me letters addressed to someplace
and they always went someplace else.*

BB GUNS

There was the time
that Clem fought back.
Bob, Chuck and Ed tried to suffocate him
underneath a stack of gunny sacks,
held them down over his face and laughed
with the derision that only children can muster.
He fought his way out, found a pitchfork
and said he'd kill all of them, and they believe
to this day, he would have tried, if their dad
hadn't stepped around that corner
when he did.

THEY WERE TOUGH LITTLE KIDS.

Chuck used to tell the others

they could shoot him

with the BB gun for a quarter.

Twenty-five cents a pop.

Or if that wasn't

attractive, a whack with a belt.

They laugh about it now, cannot believe

their foolishness. One starts out his stories

with "You can believe this or not . . ."

MOM TELLS about the time they pushed her

off the bridge at Reike's Creek,

said they'd teach her how to swim.

Angry that she was there, the only girl,

otherwise they could have been skinny-dipping.

When she went down for the fourth time

and didn't come back up,

they figured they'd better fish her out,

find a way to keep her from telling the folks.

Even now, when she thinks of water,

she still imagines it dark and muddy

over her head.

. . .

WITH TEN CHILDREN, there were daredevils

set in bare backs, a boot thrown

through a guitar,

a concussion from a horse bridle swung

at the temple.

It was her turn to ride the horse.

And every one of them came to the house,

crawled there with a broken leg,

ran soaking wet from the rain barrel

where she'd been pushed head first,

walked slowly smelling of skunk.

TEN CHILDREN. Seven of them went off to war.

Seven of them returned. Eighty-two years

of military experience between them.

Three sisters who wrote letters

and lived in the background.

Reported the news but didn't make it.

Wondered what life would have been like

if they had been born sons,

if they had been raised shooting guns.

. . .

AND THERE WAS the time Tim shot a robin

off the wire out by the tool shed.

Grandpa Joe, who was separating the milk,

marched across the yard, took that gun away,

swatted Tim hard on the butt and said "Son,

you don't shoot at birds that sing songs.

Don't ever let me see you do that again."

BROTHERS IN ARMS AT QUANG TRI

He said it didn't hurt.
I said he would make it;
we both lied.
I held his head and rocked him
until he died.
--Robert M. Smith

Like a painful gift, he finds a photograph of Mac, one he hasn't seen for twenty years, but I am around asking questions

and maybe he can finally talk.

THE PICTURE CUTS OUR CONVERSATION.

We sit in the reverent quiet: he pays his respects

to the dead and I pay mine to one still living.

His face shows the despair

he has held inside for too long.

> *We were just south of the DMZ.*
> *We shared everything.*
> *I read his mail; he read mine.*
> *He bummed chocolate from me;*
> *I bummed cigarettes from him.*
> *He liked cheese; I liked peanut butter.*

He said it didn't hurt.

I said he would make it;

we both lied.

I held his head and rocked him

until he died.

I KNOW the story from another time,

but he takes off the protective cover,

holds the photo gently on the table

with both shaking hands and tells me again,

this time he bleeds too.

> *We were in Dong Ha*
> *hooking up a generator*
> *for the Marines.*
> *Charlie booby-trapped his toolbox.*
> *It seemed the whole world exploded*
> *then. His guts spilled out*
> *like giant, soft, multi-colored hoops.*

He said it didn't hurt.
I said he would make it;
we both lied.
I held his head and rocked him
until he died.

He opens the wound long enough

to ask the familiar question why?

Opens it wide enough to allow it

to begin to heal.

MISSISSIPPI MORNING

He stands
near the wisteria-covered
gate in the still dark morning,

one hand on my suitcase

the other in the past.

>   I hope I've been helpful,
>   but I want to say,
>   I feel better.
>   I haven't talked
>   about any of this
>   for so long.

He remembers his hooch

in Vietnam, tells me

about the trench under his bed.

> At the sound of that siren
> you'd grab your gun and roll off,
> down into the hole and I tell you--
> nothing else felt as secure
> as that three foot trench--Charlie
> had to hit directly on top of your head
> to get you, I mean
> it could happen
> but your odds were damn good there.
> Standing in your underwear
> in that dirt hole
> narrower than a grave.

He rolls his tongue over his teeth,

takes a deep breath

and looks out past my shoulder.

> Then you stand there until the all clear.
> Remember that noon whistle back home?
> I was on leave once,
> walking down Main Street
> with Dad and Arvin Harris
> when that son-of-a-bitch went off.
> I dove into the gutter
> and covered my head with my hands.
> When I realized-- when I remembered
> where I was-- I got up feeling like a fool,
> but Dad and Arvin

just kept on talking
like nothing had happened.
I'll never forget that.
I tore the knees out
of a brand new pair of pants,
I went down so hard.

COWBOY IN ALASKA

"I don't have no war stories.

I was a short timer," Tim says,

that laughter loose in the top of his throat.

He stands at the forge,

pulls down his goggles

and places the horseshoe

in the red heat glow.

We grew up together and now

he shows me his life,

walks me down to the trout stream

which winds behind his house

and surrounds the cabin

in peaceful sound all summer.

"I ain't got much to say, Kate.

I hope you ain't disappointed."

We talk about the older boys

going off to war,

about losing his mother

when he was only eleven,

about Charlie's death last fall.

"Charlie taught me how to ride.

He never let on to most people

who he really was, but I knew.

He was always there for me. You know,

I bet I could say something important

about Charlie, if I put my mind to it

and maybe you gave me a little help."

TALKING TO ANGELS

In the clay red of dusk,
as light sifts down the hills
behind the barn,

he sits with his coffee cup

and watches sparrows

rest on the wire.

The same birds

built nests in the windmill

fifty years ago.

He frames his life

by the kitchen window,

looks south past the silo's sign,

"Smith and Sons" repainted

even after the boys left home

and the fields became someone else's.

A mare still grazes near the fence,

head down, content in sweet grass.

The sunset soaks into the iris of his eye

as he leans toward eighty.

"Well, good night then. See you tomorrow,"

he says out loud and no one answers or

the answer is clear and comforting

and the voice of someone dear.

SHARP SHOOTER

He led 2,000 men
In the Marines Fifth Division.
Hit the six-inch bullseye 197 times out of 200.
Hit the black circle from 200 yards away.
A native of the South Dakota prairie,
Charlie was 18 years old and 126 pounds.
He shot better than 2,000 other young men
But never told me that story,
Just left that trophy on his dresser
All those years.
I tried to interview him, but Charlie
Wasn't one for convention or bragging.
Looked at me most of my life
Through a screen of smoke.

Squinted and smiled. *Ain't that right, Kate?*

Ain't that right? He's gone now

And I'm past forty, a niece with graying hair

And growing children of my own.

I try on his dress uniform jacket,

Still on a hanger in the hollow closet.

It is too tight in the shoulders and chest.

We are saying good-by to the family farm.

Grandpa died in March and we come together

For all the right reasons.

Together, this family is stronger than any event.

I pay attention to the trophy's significance now,

Write down the details

as another uncle repeats them.

Write notes on the back

of an old Christmas card.

Happy Holidays. Wish you were here.

FOLLOW UP

There you have it, then.
    Do you remember yourselves
this way?
Is the light by the door bright enough
to find the late night steps? I have
tried to tell the story again.
Heads of State are designing new wars
even as I write; I see
this soldiering can be a lifetime job.
You all came home alive, Uncles,
and I asked you
how it felt to be young men
going off to war.
Now the wars go on without you.

Night walks slowly on the farm,

everything aches

like overused muscles. Mosquitoes buzz

near the open bulb by the front door.

Crickets carry me back years, years.

I sit on the stoop, hold this paper,

and tell you I have been listening;

I have been writing it all down.

ACKNOWLEDGMENTS

"Silk Dragons" was published in the 1991 Loft-McKnight Award anthology *Night Talk* and in *The Hermit Kingdom: Poems of the Korean War*, Kendall-Hunt Publishing, 1995.

"Talking to Angels" was published in *Threads of Experience*, an anthology from Papier-mâché Press, 1996.

ABOUT THE AUTHOR

Kathleen Patrick is a poet and fiction writer with an MA in Creative and Professional Writing from the University of Minnesota. Her writing has appeared in several literary and commercial magazines and twelve anthologies. Her poetry has received Honorable Mention from the Academy of American Poets. She received a Loft-McKnight Award in poetry and was a finalist in the Mentor Series in both poetry and fiction. Her poetry has also received support from the Jerome Foundation. She was once the hula hoop champion of Osceola County.

The audiobook version of AIRMAIL, A Story of War in Poems was recorded at Gecko Park. Special thanks to Jeff Farias, Tammy Patrick, and Bob Terhaar.

It was my dream to record the book and it started me on this publishing journey. Both the audiobook and the ebook are also available at Amazon.com

PLEASE REVIEW THIS BOOK!

I decided to finally get AIRMAIL published because I believe the stories are important. With that in mind, I would love as large a readership as possible. Reviews help get the book before more potential readers. If you enjoyed reading it, please leave a short review on Amazon. It can be a few words, or a few short sentences. It would be greatly appreciated.

www.ingramcontent.com/pod-product-compliance
Lightning Source LLC
Chambersburg PA
CBHW031646040426
42453CB00006B/220